Desert
Botanical Garden

Photographs by
Adam Rodriguez and Charles Cobeen

Cover: Cowhorn Agave,
Agave bovicornuta

Mission

The Garden's commitment to the community is to advance excellence in education, research, exhibition, and conservation of desert plants of the world with emphasis on the Southwestern United States. We will ensure that the Garden is always a compelling attraction that brings to life the many wonders of the desert.

Introduction

The Desert Botanical Garden is an oasis of beauty—a tranquil island of desert preserved within the bustling metropolis of Phoenix, Arizona. Nestled near the red rock buttes of Papago Park, the Garden is filled with one of the world's finest collections of desert plants.

Strolling through the Garden awakens the senses to new expressions of beauty. Nature's sun-warmed palette of soft green hues changes texture and form from one turn of the path to the next. Stately columns of saguaro cactus tower above spiny clusters of golden barrels. A whiptail lizard rustles the desert floor as she darts on her daily rounds. Trilling verdins and cooing doves make lilting conversation in a canopy enlivened by splashes of red, orange, and magenta blooms.

The unique beauty and exotic life forms of the area inspired a small group of Phoenicians in 1934 to form the Arizona Cactus and Native Flora Society. They wanted to preserve at least a portion of the natural desert habitat. Fired by the determination and leadership of founders Gertrude Divine Webster, an influential winter visitor, and Gustaf Starck, a local water engineer and cactus expert, the Society began to realize its dream: It founded the Desert Botanical Garden. The Garden was officially dedicated on February 12, 1939, with the bold mission to educate, research, exhibit, and conserve desert plants of the world. Its first plantings were hundreds of cactus and desert plants from the private collections of members of the Society as well as plants salvaged from mining operations.

Immediately the Garden faced significant struggles as the country suffered through the Great Depression followed by years of war. There were financial difficulties, changes in directors, jackrabbits ravaging plants, and the domestic deprivations caused by World War Two. During the war, carefully planted beds were destroyed when nearby military units dragged field guns through the Garden and shelled the area for target practice. War-torn and neglected, the Garden eventually closed.

Thankfully, a few dedicated volunteers used their gas rations to drive to the Garden and water what plants they could. The loyal efforts of those volunteers kept important pieces of the Garden's collection alive. When the war ended, only a handful of members and surviving plants were left to grow the Desert Botanical Garden into the future.

The years since the war have seen rebuilding followed by steady growth. A succession of directors, scientists, staff, and volunteers has nurtured the garden—one plant, exhibit, and educational program at a time—into a source of local pride and a popular destination for visitors from around the world.

Today the Garden is a thriving attraction that offers enlightening and inspiring experiences to more than 280,000 visitors each year. One of only forty-four botanical gardens accredited by the American Association of Museums, this one-of-a-kind museum showcases fifty acres of beautiful outdoor exhibits. The Living Collection displays the diversity of more than 50,000 desert plants and is home to 139 rare, threatened, and endangered plant species from around the world.

A charter member of the national Center for Plant Conservation, the Garden is dedicated to saving America's endangered plants through its seed bank and propagation programs. Two of the Garden's collections—the Living Collection and the herbarium—are known internationally as important resources for scientific research.

The Garden's award-winning educational programs, guided tours and seasonal events make it fun for visitors of all ages to explore and learn about the desert.

Saguaro (Crested), *Carnegiea gigantea*

Parry's Agave, *Agave parryi*

Aloe beds in bloom

House Finch

Golden Barrel, *Echinocactus grusonii*

Starfish Flower, *Stapelia* sp.

Monks' Hood Cactus, *Astrophytum ornatum*

Sea Urchin Cactus, *Echinopsis* sp.

Arizona Pincushion, *Mammillaria grahamii*

Papago Butte from the Harriet K. Maxwell Desert Wildflower Trail

Overleaf: Beavertail Prickly-pear,
Opuntia basilaris

Agave marmorata

Gila Woodpecker

17

Buckeye Butterfly

Desert Spiny Lizard

Rock Squirrel

Overleaf: Saguaro (Crested), *Carnegiea gigantea*

20

Engelmann's Prickly-pear, *Opuntia engelmannii*

Lady Finger Cactus, *Echinocereus pentalophus*

Western Screech-Owl

Echinopsis

Giant Swallowtail

Overleaf: Pages 24/25
Crested Saguaro at sunset

Julia Butterfly

Saguaro flowers, *Carnegiea gigantea*

Saguaro flower, *Carnegiea gigantea*

White-winged Dove

Mammillaria magnimamma crested

Aloe dorotheae

Webster Auditorium lit with holiday luminarias

Las Noches de las Luminarias

Turk's Head Cactus, *Melocactus pachyacanthus*

Flower of Claret-cup Cactus, *Echinocereus triglochidiatus*

Right: Pyrrhuloxia on Chuparosa,
Justicia californica

Prickly-pear flower

Blueberry Cactus,
Myrtillocactus geometrizans

Echinopsis huascha var. *rubra*

Overleaf: Echinopsis flower,
Echinopsis sp.

39

Sea Urchin Cactus, *Echinopsis* spp.

Overleaf: Senita Cactus,
Pachycereus schottii

Echinopsis huascha var. *rubra*

Beavertail Prickly-pear, *Opuntia basilaris*

Gila Woodpecker

Arizona Queen of the Night, *Peniocereus greggii*

Overleaf: Echinopsis flower

Yerba Mansa, *Anemopsis californica*

Boojum, *Fouquieria columnaris*

Cactus wren

Gambel's Quail